when I am yes

when I am yes

cin salach

JackLeg Press | Chicago | 2014

For more information on this book or to order, visit
www.jacklegpress.com

Published by

JackLeg Press
5048 N Marine Drive E6
Chicago, IL 60640

ISBN-13: 978-1492755128
ISBN-10: 1492755125

Library of Congress Cataloging-in-Publication Data

Cover painting by Lisa Villa-Moser.

Author photo by Laura Brown.

Thank you to the Ragdale Foundation where many of these poems were conceived and revised, and also to the editors of the journals in which these first appeared:

Columbia Poetry Review: "evolution"
Great Weather for Media: "April"
Court Green: "A Wide Arc"
Off the Rocks: "Buzzard's Bay"
Fifth Wednesday: "Delicious Gone"
Her Mark: "Your hands"
Windy City Queer: "January"
After Hours: "My Plans for Today"
Qarrtsiluni: "November"
Hysteria: "Women," "The Glass Girl"

Infinite gratitude to Maureen, Emily B., Lenora, MB, Melanie, the a-ville mamas (and Kelly), Sheila, Jennifer, Julie, Aunt Bonnie, my parents, Mary and Mike, and Jen Harris, who first read these poems while the monks chanted.

Much love and gratitude to Lisa Villa-Moser and Laura Brown for their amazing art.

contents

I thank you god for this most amazing day, for the leaping greenly spirits of trees, and for the blue dream of sky and for everything which is natural, which is infinite, which is yes.

- e.e. cummings

For Leo, my yes.

i.

EVOLUTION

It's Thursday and someone's testing the new church bells
so every few minutes it's Sunday.
God's in the air and out of the blue

I'm moved to begin tracking my religion
in feathers. Watch them float randomly down,
land randomly here. Looking up to witness

their journey, I'm surprised how far
they've traveled in seven days,
God's breath sending them down, establishing faith

and gravity. A noticeable pile has collected
at my feet. Proof we didn't crawl out of the ocean
in the beginning. In the beginning we just fell

out of the sky squawking, flopping, wondering
about the architecture of nests,
looking for the right building materials

and something to hold us all together.
Something like skin.
Or skin.

ii.

APRIL

1

I miss the stones

      so you are my window now.

Hand in hand we step across Melanie's backyard over cans of
      green peas

hidden in green grass, gaze at green leaves in green trees

Now I just let it water.

2

Things I do in secret:

Things I do in public:

Frankenstein's head is a stick of incense and my heart is on fire and
yours is _____ and
I don't know if I can keep my hands off. I don't know if
          my hands

                                        can

                keep
            if
I

move the rock
close the sky
end the endless pleading
to saints praised without question
save us save us anyone of us could save us
if we tried, but

tonight we are wordless searching for light
beneath headstones strung together
with leftover earth.

Where does the heart go after this?

Some people wear it like a scar   f.

3

Correspondence is not finding me walls are not knocking me down
can you hear me I said mail is not reaching me phone calls are not
ringing my voice fades the second it leaves my mouth

I don't know when it will reach you. I don't know when   will
            you
                        know
reach

        I

            a. am holding in my hands something

b. am keeping something clean
c.

                    For her final departure she is a giant
                    white owl leaning slightly forward
                    into the future of sky, monstrous
                    white wings blanketing air, beating it
                    full and upward.
                                    For her final departure she is
                                    Heart burning she leans in
                    This is the only sound in the room: obscene
                    white wings flapping, overgrown
                    angel presence, why won't she leak
                    and make this a more manageable size.

4

Give up the house
Give up the red shoes
Give up the holy
Give up the spelling bee
Give up the contract
Give up the tail

Fall fall flatten down face flat to the ground
go into the ground breathe the ground eat the
ground smell the ground love the ground

Love is the only thing that is becoming familiar.

There are twelve pages of April.

5

Still the pigeons, still the walk, the feathers, still the sidewalk curving
away, still the bare patches clenching hand hollow stomach still
              here I am with my souvenir penny, my balloon

There are hundreds of ways to kneel and kiss the ground.
There are hundreds of ways to kiss and kneel the ground.
There are hundreds of kisses to way and kneel the ground.
There are hundreds of kneels to kiss and way the ground.

What law am I breaking by getting out of bed
each morning, fur-bodied, twitching at
insect sounds, watery air, dripping leaves.

How will I bury myself, what should I wear
when the dirt drops on my head like a baptism,
sign from god, thorn in my cap, drop of blood

and all the drops dropping until there is a pool
of blood, row into the middle of the lake which is
lake blood, and I swim until red is blue and small

silvery breaths slip in and out of my mouth like fish
biting at my gums, my soft pink tissue, my old food
silly lips, cast line, I am back to the wet world.

LANGUAGE ENTERS

Awake, I
go into
the day's
life with
empty pockets
and a
clean mouth,

beg my
skin to
start talking
back, raise
words inside
like legible
welts on
the surface
of me.

After a week near the water, generations
of stones surround me and I spend days
matching each to flesh. I follow the cairns
placed on my desk and read what I write
back to the great lake. The next morning
I find these words on the beach: weapons
grandma skin pulse circle circle bird.

1. a dangerous gleam of steel
2. flames jump out the window but I never see them land
3. her absence kisses like steam
4. see-through like glass like the heart inside the head of the house inside the house
5. Small fish continue to function as the currency of intimacy before and during copulation.
6. water reveals her skin
7. 'I am a landscape,' he said, 'a landscape and a person walking in that landscape'
8. (I scream too small for my fear ah ah oh never loud)
9. to begin to like birds would be like changing religions.
10. I am the boy I am the girl I am the boy I am the girl
11. The eggs are contained in a shallow depression formed by the female as she pivots her breast in sand we are agricultural wonders cold streaks of sun drying us into stiff lines of twos, threes
12. read this with your hands behind your back, using only your nose to turn the pages.
13. like a child able to look at the true thing straight on.

Take what's in the middle
                my odd dream
                my odd forgettable dream
                my odd forgettable
my gertrudian comfort
liver heart spine

                        o
where is my
    penny in a bottle
where is my
    backyard
                how old am I really?

Let the ghosts be the ghosts
let me not have conversations with the ghosts
                go to bed with the ghosts
    do laundry for the ghosts
                jump out of the way for the ghosts.

For my birthday, my friend gives me a fossil of a jelly fish from
Mazon Creek, a dig site in southern Illinois. Her husband's an
archeologist. The fossil has been on their back porch for two years
and just split open this morning. He tells her Mazon Creek is one of
the only places in the world that preserves soft-bodied things. She
tells me Mazon Creek is one of the only places in the world that
preserves soft-bodied things. I write it down like it is gospel: Mazon
Creek is one of the only places in the world that preserves soft-
bodied things. The fossil is 290 million years old. I am 41

        my red bike in the yard next to the porch,
        small sprouts of green rising.

BUZZARD'S BAY

The stillness here moves me
        I see the glass
negative crash of the flat bay
        I see it is stone
 I lay myself in a sky as flat as the bay
        I pick up each stone and hold it in my mouth
nothing is moving
        I learn all the stones on the shore
but I am flying
        I come to the shore
the tide makes its way to the rock
        I sell the house
the rock makes its way to the body
        I relinquish the keys
the body makes its way to her
        negotiating
I say yes.

Here is my nose my elbow my grief
here is my molar my cheekbone my crazy
here is my spine my buttocks my anger
here is my belly my thigh my sweet
here is my ankle my shoulder my thinking
here is my help my hard my hair
here is my hamstring my vocal my thumb
here is my bladder my eyes my fail
here is my hysteria my old my moon
here
      is my baby.

My dreams bring me down to the water. If I close
my eyes after waking, the images come back—
I am scrambling down a hill to reach the water.
I am climbing over hundreds of sunbathers
to reach the water. I am running away from
my brother father husband to reach the water.
I am ignoring all posted signs to reach the
water, and when I reach the water it's daylight,
but the water's so dark. I find a place I know
is safe and slip in. I swim well, efficient and
slippery, but always on the lookout, always
peering under with my goggles, keeping an eye
on the shore, horizon, rock that might not really
be a rock. I swim, and I keep swimming until

I am awake.

To make something with your own hands
to love your body
to see the body of the one you love.
To make something with your own hands
to love your body
to want the body of the one you love.
To make something with your own hands
to love your body
to touch the body of the one you love.
To make something with your own hands
to love your body
to feed the body of the one you love.
To make something with your own hands
to love your body
to taste the body of the one you love.
To make something with your own hands
to love your body
to know the body of the one you love.
To make something with your own hands
to love your body
to love the body of the one you love.

DELICIOUS GONE

*For the inaugural exhibition...the artist Emily Katrencik is
eating the wall that separates the gallery space from the
bedroom of its director, Louky Keijsers.*
--New York Times, February 2005

It's a process only a woman could conceive, a hungry woman, because
every woman answers to hunger. What we feed our bones, what we
slave and give away. Our intimacy comes with tiny teeth marks and
we like it that way. We build small rooms then eat them slowly.
Digestion = privacy. That calcium sulfite is an ingredient of drywall is
a bonus.

I didn't plan on eating everything on my plate. It was in the
way of the table. Which was in the way of your lap.

I imagine the breaking through, what it might taste like. I pretend it
in my mouth. Last gasp of wall then holy roundness of nothing. First
crumble of exposure. *I prefer cast concrete. It has a more permanent
flavor. You can taste the iron.* Women can't get enough iron, I read.
Monthly bleeding makes it popular.

There is nothing between us you won't smell on my breath,
eventually.

This is what we look like when we're eating: Flushed and focused.
Flagrant. *I'm better at taking things away.* Confession = digestion. We
are full of evidence. We are genius bulimics. Sculptors of absence.
Delicious gone.

Stop the fear that steam rolls under your skin, leaving black question marks like infection waiting to ruin your day. Intersect heavy machinery, sabotage its path, slash the cables, put nails in the tires, sugar in the gas tank. Be part he, part she, the smell of my breath changing from pears to cigars depending on what you're wet for. Carry an ocean in me always, in case you want to bathe in salt or search for stones, sea singing you from flesh to fin while ancient stars surface and shine.

CHELSEA

The day we arrive I feel lean and long and able to leap big bridges in single nights as long as the lights invite me back to the pretty side, the humming city side that is not mine but yours and so I love it. It's my step city. I send it postcards at holidays and sometimes just for fun. Tomorrow let's go see the zoo. You carry the camera, I'll carry the water, we'll both carry on like we haven't seen each other in weeks in cities but really we have. We woke up together just this morning in the perfect room in the perfect hotel with the peeping fern that matches the curtains when the light hits them from behind. And it is perfect except for no pay-per-view, so we drag the carpet onto the fire escape and find another view. We eat and then we kiss. We think about fucking and then get sensible. That happens a lot with us. Fucking sensible.

The next day I echo you echo you dykes marching down fifth and I am amazed at the estrogen-ish energy, great haircuts, my desire to be only this only this and I don't know how to eat this anger so I fly away let you find me on a New York bed sheer-y curtains loose skirts no underwear, we empty ourselves of words, fill ourselves on body, and it feels so good I don't know anything I know more. Then train and mango and you all over my skin and who is this dark Hudson calling you always.

The drive back is history of sand, hotel swimming and we are two little girls, too little but still this burning underneath, this waiting flight, and all the way home I want you all the way home to open me reach inside, and when we arrive your bed feels like our bed and we shed everything. After that everything flies and so do I to another bed on another side of town and the next morning you wake up missing and I wake up

Slow voluntary change.

A small thing on a big thing

                          a fairy on a god

        a bird on a planet

                anything mid-   air.

For one brief moment there is
a plane full of people in my mouth, waiting
for me to speak, sit, rollover.

An earthquake followed by a buffalo woman.

A good card for womyn who work with fire.

Sunday is on the other side of a room filled with eggshells.

(hora, amazon, pan, bast, manipulation, temperance, yemaya, chantico,
cerridwen, storm, kali, the learner, yemaya, shakti, the rattle, the witch,
spiderwoman, moo, compassion, pasowee, victory, deception, mami watu,
victory, conflict, ecstasy)

We switch sides of the bed and do it again.

Follow the sounds to the next layer, sing
"take me out." Here is the home run,
here is the American baseball pie, the rope
to hang myself out to dry.

Things could not be easier, that is the news
from the home front, things could not be easier.

So take the money and run.
Take the honey and gun.
Take the bunny and nun.

She goes away for so long, for so long she is gone.

rush my skin like rivers. Fish jump my belly, lay their eggs and continue downstream. Your breathing brings rain and even the ocean watches you move. You don't understand why I have such a hard time sometimes, storms that leave me for drowning, clogging the current like so many wet leaves, rearranging creeks and poems. You live with a clear blue conscience, swaying in your own big breeze singing, it's so good to be here be here. be here. I listen as faithfully as an atheist, knowing how much you can accomplish when you are not waiting around for miracles. And then it happens, small as a word, loud as the truth, all that knowledge comes crashing into question and my true nature is revealed: I'm a believer

I couldn't leave her if I tried.

MAY

A woman coming out of marriage
asks if it's supposed to be this hard
and I pull the water over us
like a blanket.
We are amazing daughters,
we are amazing daughters.

(a row of huts)
(a city of women)

Work comes from the body and the body moves
into it like a vessel.

(a clump of bunks)
(a tower of toilets)

Fill me with work.

The roads are closed I cannot go down those roads again the roads
are closed the roads are really closed I cannot go down those roads
again they are really closed really the roads are closed they are really
closed the roads are really closed.

It's Sunday and I am in a field of women. When I swing,
the meeting of ball and bat lets out a crack and I watch
as it flies into some woman's waiting hands. I sigh when
she catches it, holds it up in victory.

I sleep approximately 8 hours each night.
I eat approximately $100 worth of food each week.
I have two cats.
I make a circle of flower petals on my desk.
I steal an orange poppy.

None of it was a mistake.

Everything whipping
by me and me slow in the
  middle, wondering

if she might want to kiss me
when my mouth thaws into spring.

If I wear vast wings and large flight and take up the entire sky with my flapping and do not make myself small even for god.

If I hold myself above myself no longer child no longer adolescent humming through cemeteries for original dates of birth.

If I open my body to earth's tongue the snakes' striptease unafraid to watch myself split in two revealing you and you.

If I welcome truth like my own metallic skin saying "yes" singing the silver birds out of their nests *I a bell awakened*

If this is the question I'll ask again and again would I be good if I would I be better if I then today I won't ask.

I will transgress glass squeal with pleasure do this more than once in my lifetime.

BETWEEN

From up here the distance takes forever to travel.
On the ground I walk with my tongue between my legs.
How long have I been this woman? How many times
have I given this number out?

The lessons are my spine my basement my shoes.
Words are watermarks I check every few days
to see how high I've risen, how low I've sunk.
The air feels like something less than salvation. Skin
is my salvation. Glass is my light my revealer my spy.

I am lying on the bedroom floor rising up, skin slipping off me like
bedcovers and I am inflating myself with my own breath, ascending
like a phoenix in Macy's

Thanksgiving Day parade, all these ropes attached to all these hands,
attached to all these bodies holding tight as we maneuver me down
the street ho! ho! It is a parade of me

and I am laughing out loud, I am so big there is not enough room for
both of us and as he vanishes into the universe I let go as fast as I
can, open my hands my inside places

my hiding spaces, let them fall fifty one hundred ten thousand feet,
let them drop from the highest point I've ever been, they are my
original sin, taking their own sweet time and I am in no hurry

floating down fifth avenue, bouncing between buildings, released
from a stranger's skin I am my own next of kin.

There were two roads I instinctively walked down/
didn't walk down, in the beginning there were two roads
and instinctively I counted them, one two one two
I counted them in the beginning there were two roads
and I walked down them/didn't walk down them
instinctively, one two one two, there were.

WORSHIP

Inhale when the glass invites me in
singing, swim through fire to save me.
Exhale and hold perdition between

my lips. Kiss god in the face of god
and picture old nick plump with pleasure.
Look up profane, circle pew, pulpit,

preacher, penance, believe all I need
to turn temple into pagoda is desire.
Repeat until the pope pops in to see

if I'm up for a little communion, but
confess that I just ate the body of god
an hour ago, so I'm not hungry yet.

People who pray in glass churches
shouldn't worship stones.

I've wanted to live in a glass house as long as I can remember.
The idea of it thrilled me. I had a million questions for my mom
but got it down to three: Would the bathroom be glass too?
Could people see everything always or would there be one room
in the house that wasn't glass? What about when you sleep—
could people watch you dream?

The ocean in my body moves and the world rocks itself awake,
rested, smooth, sleep shakes its hair loose falling open around my
mouth making me an easy entrance for all visitors. It's a free day. The
moon is handing out afternoon passes and this is not a fantasy but I
dreamed it once while I was swimming long laps through the lake
pretending ocean and imagining water's entrance, a billion airless

doorways swinging wide from Chicago to Laguna, the breathless
Caribbean, the busy Gulf. And I was balancing my body on lake
currents, surfing right below the surface of me, my line of flesh blood
bone thinking fish be fish, slip through, when the glass entered my
mind, the crucible of sand, 2000 degrees of ambition and accidents
and all my air floated to the surface.

After gathering and marver-ing and blowing.
After reheating and blocking and necking.
After filing and tapping and transferring.
After jax-ing and flashing and breaking, this:

Stand back. Kneel.
Enter yourself like a house.

JULY

Whatever your heart clings to and confides in, that is really
your god.

- Martin Luther

When I return home
my clothes are covered
in a fine layer of glass dust.
My shirt catches the light,
my jeans sparkle.

Before I come out
before the story comes out
before words loosen
before skin slips
before heat enters
before

glass is my god
my skirt shines.

The square root of purple
is white.

Today I crave the fleshiest part of
the landscape, the body in the landscape,
the light on this particular day
burying the body in the landscape.

I measure the velocity of shadows
in words, in letters home, as the light
begins to echo itself, ball-of-fire
toward the speck of myself I become

on earth from sky, burying itself in
me so deep, I place slivers of sun like
wafers on my tongue and pray high.

At 2000 degrees
glass gives you
no resistance.

Like water, you could
be inside and not
                    even know.

I am elemental in this new home of bones
and air, tending my mouth, waiting for
someone to speak me, match each word
to a grain of sand, hear the heat of language

begin it's inevitable crack and send me
spiraling into the skin of the universe, which
is made of glass, so every god can quickly
note discrepancies and disenchantments.

It is possible to cut a sheet of glass to any desired
shape with an ordinary pair of scissors, if the operation
is performed under water. A smooth edge cannot
be obtained by such means, but it will be found satisfactory.

The furnace enters me,
becomes the bowl

of my body,
glass mouth singing.

Every 2000 degrees, something.
The formula for this?

Weather choosing
tiny wings, flight.

These are the things I reach back for:
music, mouths, poppies, sun.
Even as I write this I know some things are missing:
patents, progress, certain birds.

Music, mouths, poppies, sun
open the body in similar ways.
Patents, progress, certain birds
leave the body in similar states,

open the body in similar ways,
revealing light and seed, the formula for glass.
Leave the body in similar states;
dusted with sand, transparent in some places.

Revealing light and seed, the formula for glass
is found in *Henley's Twentieth Century Book*
        of Ten Thousand Formulas
(dusted with sand, transparent in some places)
among recipes for hair tonic and violet water.

Found in *Henley's Twentieth Century Book*
        of Ten Thousand Formulas,
the formula for glass does not vary much
from recipes for hair tonic and violet water—
exact in their measure, certain of their outcome.

The formula for glass does not vary much –
sand, ash, calcium, heat,
exact in their measure, certain of their outcome –
from the first formula, before science, tablespoons.

Sand, ash, calcium, heat
earth, ocean, air, fire—
the first formula—before science, tablespoons,
before glass, before skin.

Earth, ocean, air, fire—
even as I write this I know some things are missing:
before glass, before skin.
These are the things I reach back for.

Spell for the Undoing of Prayers

Let go the hands that fold me, let go the tongue that tells me
the trees the creek, they know, they will speak me now

Let go the house that holds me, let go the family that calls me
the moon the sun, they know, they will hear me now

Let go the name that follows me, let go the voice that carries me
the ocean the stones, they know, they will sing me now

Let go the sex that begins me, let go the veil that becomes me
the ground the breeze, they know, they will reveal me now

I leave   my signs of leaving spread neatly across the floor
                             announcing *I'm leaving*

       to architect my own body

in the smooth ache of arch and bridge   the red belly of fly
and seed green of water   gold of wind
        stillness of pine and stone   crawl of light.

I'm leaving

                   to hear my
              own body answer:

       she is a wave, all the rest is negotiable.

DECEMBER

Songs swan and swoon.
I am not sure how to dance abandon,
tame gin.
To just float on my back breathing is new.
I am still unknowing this.
Flowers are next.
3   two   one
I am moving! I come apart!

WOMEN

bend over black patches, let go seeds into
ripe piles of earth, wait for forests to grow.
Witch into groups of three or more singing,
this city is a cauldron. Damp shadows

dripping from the moon, we ghost into being
then wander into other forms: honey
pots jelly jars bed posts. Bump our heads on
low things; ceilings stairs knees desire. Crawl

when fragrant gullies of light call to us
in low, bass-y moans; women, women
live quiet like fish live quiet in rivers,
like tornadoes live quiet in cornfields

in August. Nameless cones spinning across
weather maps movie screens hotel beds, we
sandwich hours between sheets, delay maids
with days of "please do not disturb", evoke

sound from places that otherwise have none:
tree limbs parking lots straight-backed chairs. Women
become in a silence only we know
how to break: now the air now the air, now.

THE GLASS GIRL

Once upon a time I was a little girl who lived in a glass house.
The house was my body, my skin enclosed in the thinnest layer of
glass imaginable. From a distance you couldn't even tell, the glass was
so smooth. People liked the way I shined in the light & said I must be
special. I moved slowly, lady-like, always careful where I sat or slept
for fear I'd break the glass.

Years passed without a scratch. Then I started to grow & once or
twice someone got too close & I broke. Each time I stitched the glass
pieces back together. After a while my body became a translucent
quilt of nerves & flesh. I looked in the mirror & thought "monster."

My handsome heart, stranger skin.
My experimental love.

I put my vibrating penis back in the drawer. I know there are men in the world, but I've yet to find one who vibrates. I expect things to be hard. I pay extra for them to vibrate.

Women vibrate hard and I want that about them. They shake and shimmer everything into electricity. Men? Slippery with savior. Mine. And theirs. Who can resist?

Have you heard the one about the girl who really wants a boy but ends up with me? Have you heard the one about the boy who really wants a girl but ends up with me?

A healer once told me I was a threshold for gender. A window boy/girl could slip in and out of to explore the other side. I was both. Never neither.

Out of context I am content. There is an explanation for everything and it's too bad because it's much more interesting when there's not. Take now.

WHEN I AM YES

This is why we love the mid-west:

Because with our eyes closed

Because the warm cool belly

Because when there are women

Because someone else's version of the sky

Because everything is part massacre

Because our most dark and leafy places

Because when the big boulder of winter

I see a feather land in a window
and it's the kind of window that opens out
like a bin. I'm about to reach in when
a tiny lion appears and bites my finger.

Later at the gift shop, the woman
at the register offers me flowers
and I am elated. Leaving,
I spot the feather in the store-front window.

Because I grab it like I'm stealing

Sometimes I feel like a curve-billed thrasher,
ten and a half inches long, spotting on my upper breast,
orange eye foraging for seeds, my nest of leaves
lined with horsehair, rootlets and placed

in a thorny bush high above the ground.
But on long, slow mid-west mornings like these
I am almost always found in large flocks
that feast on small fruit, my voice

a repeated high-pitched buzzy trill.

1.

It's a Kenny Loggins concert in sign language and Bob Dylan is wandering through the audience singing. It doesn't look like him or sound like him so I'm surprised it is him. I want to say something but don't really know much about his music so I keep to myself.

2.

I'm running through the parking lot and it's dark so I don't notice that mine is the only car left and I'm about to get in, turn the ignition, when I notice all my doors are wide open. I look around. No one. I start to close each door but before I can reach the last one, a strange car pulls up right next to me and I get that feeling in my stomach like

3.

We are in Greece watching a family of four try to raise their car from out of the water. From where we're standing they look like giant sea monsters, but then the scale returns to normal and their car rises to the surface. It's a blue Jeep Cherokee.

4.

We are pulling the airplane behind us the way a child pulls a toy train, cars bobbing one behind the other

5.

I throw my fear into the lake—a blessing of beads, a crush of sage. I throw my fear into the lake and it swirls in the February rage of Lake Michigan. Then I sit in the shower and turn my fear into a country song.

6.

My baby is tiny as a moth, or Tinkerbelle. I am happy to have her but it seems too early, like I got her too soon. Sometimes she's a kitten, but mostly she's a baby and I have no idea how to take care of her and feel very guilty and very alert. I keep her in the top drawer of my grandma's dresser on a little heating pad and check frequently to make sure she's breathing but sometimes it's very hard to tell. Later while driving, I see broken animals and they are gruesome. The first is a black standard size poodle broken in half, but there are others, half-beaten, half-bloody walking down the road in the opposite direction from me. The last animal I see is a rhino. It's whole.

7.

I score poems while watching the Olympics. The skater from Russia
just landed her triple Lutz and although she has never been known
for her artistry (according to the German judge) her blue skating
outfit sparkles, glistening.

Black balloons floated down like flocks of birds. White stuff fell from another part of the sky and I ran to the door and screamed "let me out." The backyard was bigger

than I remembered. I slipped down the porch like it was a slide and went to see the white stuff which turned out to be giant pieces of shredded paper. Even though it was winter

I had no coat and as I walked further from the house I noticed a river and thought how lucky to have a house next to a river. My dog ran over and a woman crawled

across the yard toward a baby boy she said she was watching for her sister. The baby was crying but implied in baby talk that he wanted my necklace, the beaded one.

I saw he was already wearing a few so I put mine around his neck and he calmed down. The dog curled in my lap while I patted the baby's back and feeling very content I said

to the woman, "I never knew there was a river here" and just then tracks started appearing and she said "I don't think there is a river here, it's flooded from the snow"

and as my dog ran toward the water I heard a train coming and screamed his name but it came out soft like a whisper and I moved in slow slow motion.

The grass is alive under this small bowl of dirt, stones stand guard and she is out there with her warm breath and god hands, and my body is not afraid.

Yesterday at the Everglades my parents took us on an airboat ride and halfway through the ride the driver of the boat (not my father) took a sharp turn, startling a bird mid-air

and the bird flew right into my chest. That evening after dinner as I walk to my father's car, I notice a dead bird stuck to his fender. I show it to my mom who waits patiently

while I place it in a nest of grass next to the strip mall where the restaurant is.

For if god is not curled up in my chest, then she is surely swimming in the trees that meet the path that watches from my window.

It has something to do with the back of my throat ready to offer up a song or breakfast, and out of it comes voracious pretentious luscious words I cannot use ever, but can leave here knowing I am capable of leaving what I once considered unleavable.

CLOSE

Morning happens over and over throughout the night and you are
waking into it, your new brightness, your holy dark. Today's god is 70
threads reaching back and pulling you forward one at a time, and I
become a witness to the effect of translucence, how it dissolves solid
into essence; the skin of god. I believe science is faith with numbers
and I believe in faith, which should feel redundant, but doesn't. Today
it is the spine of time and I wander its labyrinth willingly, wandering
close enough to hear the swish of something, the ground maybe, as it
softens into something as open and terrifying as love.

THIS DAY

Like my dream last night where my ex-husband and I were denied
passports and he was very upset and ready to do battle but I didn't
really care that much until someone (not my ex-) decided to force the
issue and threaten the messenger (a woman—Asian? Russian?) of the
denied passport news by holding a gun to her throat and I was so
appalled at this behavior, even for a dream, I said enough. Are you
serious? I'm waking up.

I'm afraid of swimming in the ocean diving head first into raucous
waves the unknown terror of the undertow and getting body
slammed back into the beach oh I do it head right in fear riding high
on my shoulders fearless friends laughing the look on my face saying
fun! And I surface through that first wall of water the buoyancy of
salt calms me and I think you know maybe it's not so maybe I've
maybe and then the tower of water building height on the horizon
fearless friends yelling *this is the one this is one* my heart pounding
the theme song from Jaws my dog-paddle-point-of-view confirming
that this is the biggest wave I've ever seen anyone's ever seen. Is
anyone seeing this? *This one is yours!*

I am eating the perfect breakfast of peaches and raspberries from a
milk glass bowl translucent enough for the sun to light its thick
whiteness which I witness after I walk away to get a scarf and a book
of poetry and when I get back I see my bowl on the end of the pier
illuminated from inside marinated in sun and sky and when the wind
stops for 5 seconds or especially a couple of minutes the sudden
stillness of warmth graces my entire body and everything and nothing
feels this good the lake neighbor's dog starts barking barely audible
but I hear it and as I do I am reading a great poem about dogs
barking I write this down and wonder if we are always living in
memory and a line from another poem confirms it everything we see
is in the past, which makes me think about stars and how the only
thing I really know about them is that if I see them it means they are
dead and their dying light has taken thousands of years to reach my
eyes and I'm still not sure whether I like that fact or not I lie on my
back on the pier to lessen the wind and my back opens to the soft
wood planks I form shapes against the sky with my hands and then
as if the sky were a bowl of water I dip my hands in it's such a clear

59

clean blue and as I lift them back out a sliver of moon floats up
between my palms shocks me in that perfect way I always want to be
shocked back into life like the first breath after birth must feel like
yes quickly followed by yes

iii.

APRIL, AGAIN

Is this spring? So much water
being shuttled across the street.

And now this swooping back into whole,
heavy lungs holding up slippery heart.

The swimming, the singing.
Still so much rocking.

The white car zooming toward, white sun streaming behind, white
snow piled high all around, white clouds floating,

I am the ant guy
I am the guy who carries the rice
I am the lemonade drinking guy
I'm the guy that pushes a ball with a stick
I'm the guy who takes care of these two things.

My own passivity.
My own passiveness.
My own letting things slip.

My own.

The living room is soft in the middle now.
Anger has shipped.

Off goes the victim head!
Off goes the hard head!
On goes the me head:
complicated, clear burning, bright lighted,
holy holy head.

Eat the day.
Eat the good day.
Eat the really really really good day.
Have a good day.

Snakes could be coincidence.
Coincidence could be luck.

Next door a chicken lays an egg.

I do not have to rush things.

(Sex got smaller and smaller, until it was a slight opening, a brush
across skin. I held my breath and stared hard, trying to see, what
else? Then it closed. And I forgot.)

You count hairs until they split and then you count those.
Meanwhile mountains.
How do I not judge everything?
Eventually anger makes you ridiculous with truth.
Eventually love.

Now I am almost done with my forties.
I am almost done with my forties.
I let them go. I let them go
and they are coming up now,
like spring they are coming up
now, into fifty.

Everything shines now.
What lovely weather is this?
Your face facing mine.

E-MONKA (AN EMAIL SOMONKA)

Who landscapes the world?
Who predicts the rain, and all
that blooms, symbolic
lilac, its fragrant briefness.
What I know, a thimble full.

Some books speculate
flowering plants cultivate
beauty to increase
their survival with humans.
Take tulips for example.

Dear poet, I'm sure
singing comes first. Intention
another music
subtle in its progression,
so different than this waiting.

Ok, when totaled,
the weight of all the sunlight
that hits the earth in
a day equals the exact
weight of an ocean liner.

Have you done the math?
A basket full equals what?
A spring? A summer?
How many farms? How many
generations of reaping?

Unsure, the crow takes
two or even three wives, but
this is not a game.
He is accommodating
and admires compulsiveness.

A cockroach prefers
pressure on all sides of its
body. There is a
specific term for this, but
I cannot remember it.

I make myself write
backwards into your answer.
but the music seems
to have other plans, placing
each word like a new partner.

Bats always turn left
exiting caves, dolphins sleep
with one eye open,
mosquitoes live for fifteen
minutes, and on and on and

I ascend into
answers, the surrendering
the continuing
of the story, as I am
no longer listening.

What turns this into
conversation other than curiosity?
I send you a question and
you move from sleep to answer.

Scientists believe
human mirror cells are the
root of empathy,
bright, shiny neurons that fire
our desire to watch, mimic.

I lift you shining into the breakfast of your room, ripe pear of your changing table, oatmeal of the radiators humming. Swept out of myself, I am swept back in, dusted.

What shall we what shall we find today? Where will the path of the house lead hurray? And if we are dry and if we are brushed and if we are if we are curious enough?

Sugarplumboy you crack my mouth up. You hug my holy. You make today the only day I need. Mmmma. I surrender language. Mmmma. I adopt yours.

Bumpy-gummed dawn rises to meet plumped up and steamy such touchable sleep. What shall we wear when our morning stripes keep slipping and sliding right down to our feet?

Twelve hours of you tucked into dreaming is intoxicating. I am intoxicated. Gasping, I breathe only you. Your birth slashed me. Slashed, I gush you.

It is impossible to grieve when the sun
is shining so loudly, impossible

to carry the heaviness heavily, without
skipping, without holding it high

above my head in a brightly colored basket.
But how empty before full, how long to arrive,

how I took it by the hand and walked with it
each night, staring at the moon, pleading.

To swaddle such sadness turns it into something
else and grief has no place to nestle, poor grief.

Dear Chris,

I wrote an entire poem to you while I was checking email last night. Another while I was giving Leo a bath and reading him stories. Another after I loaded the dishwasher and pushed the start button. You would have been impressed. But I did not actually write them. They wrote themselves in and out of my head before I could find fingers pen paper and one toddler free second to bring them all together. Ah.

Dear Chris,

I just typed two lines I wished were as good as the ones in the nonexistent poems I wrote last night but they weren't so I deleted them. It is still me and you and this letter, waiting for poetry to find us.

Dear Chris,

Nothing is a clock. The middle of the night doesn't always mean sleep. The morning doesn't always mean there won't be a table full of open wine bottles on your front sidewalk. And it's Sunday. What does that mean?

Every time I start a new paragraph a little icon pops up and tells me it looks like I'm writing a letter and do I need help? No.

I just typed "letter" with three "t's" and it was corrected by my computer unprompted. Yes.

Yesterday I got an email from my oldest best friend. 44 years ago our parents bought houses across the street from each other. She wrote that the day before she had come home from running errands to find her first born son, 21 years old, dead in his room. She had the caramel ice cream that he had requested before she left. I broke into sobs. I kept breaking into them. Her tender email held me. Just last month Leo and I visited her in her suburban home. I looked at pictures of her two boys, unable to imagine Leo that big.

I remember when your girls turned two, Chris. I asked how it felt to be the father of two, two-year olds. You answered, "They're still alive." I smiled. You said, "I'm serious."

Everything is unprecedented. Everything has happened. How does that work?

It is unprecedented that I am the mama of a 20-month old boy, asleep in the next room.

This breaking is how we let the light in. That's what Leonard Cohen sings. But it's not the light I am trying to let in.

Dear Chris,

(No I don't need help writing this letter)

I once was in love with a woman who was very good at letting in the dark and she left me with some great skills for doing just that, but I've gotten rusty.

The weather today is light enough to let the dark float inside, soft and black and unflinching. I float inside both of them as I pour the unfinished wine into the sewer in our street and bag up the empty bottles. I see a small sweatshirt (boy's) and little shoes (girl's) left on different porches, memories of last night's block party. It is hard to match everything up in the pitch of darkness, especially small things to small things. Much easier to wait for the light.

waiting,
cin

How to Jump from a Bridge or Cliff into a River

1.   Be proactive—jump before anyone else has even considered it.

2. Boredom
   Anxiety
   Physical challenge
   Political refuge
   Hunger
   Everyone else is

3. Laminate these directions. Then when you encounter the occasion to jump from a bridge or cliff into a river, you'll have waterproof notes showing you how.

4. Be more sacred than scared. Bow your head, clasp your hands, hover above the water, pray: Our father, who art a river, how shallow it be? Thy name.

5. Transform from a bullet into a dragonfly.

6.   Mid-air your hair—a floating pile of flames.

7. I am jumping from my forehead into my big toe.

I am jumping from my twenties into my hundreds.

I am jumping from my coffin into my window box.

I am jumping from my confusion into my convertible.

8.

AFTER HE GOES TO BED

The horse never made it out of the stable, but
the cows are kissing and the pig is rolling

in the sheep's mud. A small spoon rests
next to the hen, who has left her eggs to play

music. The farmer is asleep in the garden,
having been flipped from his bed

by my boy, who laughed and laughed. The farmer's
dog is stuck in the hayloft but is happy with hay.

Two

The story is not real. The pirate is not real. Peter Pan is not real. I rock him until he believes I am real and trusts sleep. I rock him until sleep comes for me too, and I trust it mostly, but still it teases me the next day. *More?* It says. *Would you like some more?*

Not cruel, just real.

Today we meet a friend and her son at the beach and stay for hours. Leo wades in and out of the lake, filling a little yellow watering can, saving lady bugs, saving "another kind of bug", eating peanuts, smiling into the blowing sand when the wind picks up. I talk, I watch, I dig, I rescue balls that blow too far out. I hold my bottle of water up to his lips because his hands are too full of this day to hold anything else. I am in love. It is real.

ALICE ASKS

In the long run, are the animals wonderful?
Oh yes. A basket of plastic molded lions, panthers, elephants.
They ride the train and wander the farm, take walks to the park.

Did the machine stop working just because of me?
It's possible. Did you check the plug?

Is the moment right before the door the only thing?
Until you walk through. Then it becomes the past and so on.

Should I try to pick the ripest cherries?
Only because I know how far you think ahead do I understand your
dilemma. If you pick the ripest cherries the pleasure is immediate.

Did you see the blur just outside the window last night?
It was a blur of ripening: darkness, moon, spring.

Did you cry the last time you fell?
I wanted to, but Leo started to laugh. He thinks all falls are pratfalls
and cracks up as soon as the body lurches, bumps, loses balance. And
because I would do anything to hear him laugh like that, I did what
any mother in love with their child would do. I fell again.

He is pouting and tearing up a magazine. *The Sun.* No, *Utne.* No, *Dwell.* He is peeking around my computer. He is climbing on the radiators, out of his sleepy but not-sleepy-enough-for-a-nap-skin. *Can I stand here?* He is trying so hard. I am trying so hard. And we are doing it. We are working on doing it for 10 minutes a day. I set a timer. 10 minutes used to be nothing. Now it is a fucking retreat. I should not be typing fucking while he is staring the screen.

Can I sit next to you while you write a poem mama?
If you do not ask me any questions, yes.
I won't ask you any questions.
Ok.
Can I touch your hair?
Leo, that's a question.

He is poking my head with his foot. I don't know how much time is left on the timer. I don't know how much is left on anything. He is lying on his side and he is having a hard time. A showdown. He pushes me out of my chair. I get up and tell him the timer is being turned off and there is no popsicle. He says he will sit still and moves over. I tell him if he takes his uneaten half hot dog into the kitchen, throws it away, comes back and sits quietly, we will try again. I watch his tiny perfect body run to the kitchen and back.

Are you going to write poetry?
Yes.
I'm going to eat poetry mama!

He is sitting on the arm of the chair, next to me, naked, holding a baking sheet with pieces of rice cake. He says they are green eggs and ham. He is smiling and putting his rice cake breath right in my face. *Do you like green eggs and ham mama?* He is crunching in my ear, climbing on my head, wrapping his legs around my shoulders. Rice cake is falling down around me.

Leo, are you going to get a popsicle today?
Yes.
Have you been letting mama write quietly?
Yes.
No. You've asked for things and spilled things.
I won't spill anything mama.
If you can sit quietly next to me for 5 minutes, we can have a popsicle.
I can mama.
I think you can too.

We are sitting quietly.
I am pulling for him.
He waves to me.
He is sitting next to me waving.
What was that noise mama?
Honey, no questions until the timer goes off.

Oh Susanna, don't you cry for me, I've gone to Alabama with a banjo on my knee!

Am I big enough for gum?
No honey.
Is Ernie?
Nope.
Is Bert?
Nope.
Is my octopus?
Nope.

He stands next to my computer making music. He is doing it to bug me but he is winning me over. Now he is running to get more instruments. He is digging through his instrument basket. Ah ha! Cymbals! The loudest most annoying of all instruments! He is so proud of himself. It is a big crashing sound. Threatening and exhilarating all at once. Cymbals in my face! Cymbals in my ear! Cymbals in his mouth!

Check check, check.
I'm going to sing a song about bikes mama.
Bikes! And banjos! And tambourines! And lights!
Hey mama, where are our lights?"

The timer goes off.

It's a stupid world of haunted gossip. Whispy whispers and
sarcasm that bops you over the head when you thought you were
falling in love.

It's a ridiculous effort to walk and smile, and mean it. Anger is a
shadow that turns into peculiar weather the month before

spring. Weather that whistles happy tunes of "change is in the air"
then knocks leaves off. I type this while I have a baby in the next
room sleeping.

What is perfect? It is as big as two children pretending to be two
adults. What if I haven't written since that date?

What if it was sex? What if we haven't had sex since that date? What
if you asked? Now the river in my fingers. Now the brake lights
flashing. Now the hook

in my voice. An upset pig can sound like an upset baby.
It's easier to write when I imagine you reading it. If I eat

my macaroni I can have a cookie. If I eat my cookie, I can have a
muffin. Today we meet a boy named Huckleberry. He is

seven and wearing overalls. His mom is peaceful, hippy blonde. I
imagine becoming friends with someone like her here.

Bugs bounce off the gutters. I am trying to let go of it all but
between myself and the reflection of myself is a large stone.

Between a large stone and the reflection of myself is me. In the center
of the house sits a woman in pain and the pain radiates. The house
stretches to heal.

It's a stupid world of haunted gossip. Whispy
whispers and falling in love.

It's a ridiculous effort to walk and smile, and mean it
the month before

spring. Weather whistles happy tunes of "change is in the air"
then knocks leaves off.

What is perfect? It is as big as two children pretending.
What if it asked?

Now the river in my fingers. Now the brake lights flashing.
Now the hook

in my voice. An upset pig can sound like an upset baby.
If I eat

my macaroni I can have a cookie. Today we meet
Huckleberry. He is

seven and wearing overalls. His mom is peaceful, hippy.
We move here.

Bugs are bouncing off the gutters. I am trying to let go of it all.
Between myself and the reflection of myself is a large stone.

In the center of the house sits a woman in pain and
the pain and the house heal.

It's a stupid world of falling in love.

It's a ridiculous effort the month before.

Weather whistles then knocks leaves off.

What is perfect? It is big.

Ask the river in my fingers. The hook

in my voice. If I eat

my macaroni I can have Huckleberry. He is

seven and wearing overalls. Here

I let go.

The reflection is a large stone.

The center of the woman heals.

WHY?

Because wild bird, daily cardinal,
red, banging into a mirror.
A bag of plastic bugs.
A pinch of AC.
Two past lives caught in my throat, released.
4 angels swooping him to him.

Because a block of men and women
A gate of babbling sharks

Large amethyst
Large violet
Large silver
Lovely magenta

Because even when I find myself clinging,
even though it is cliché, I cheer the effort:
Hip hip cliché! Hip hip cliché!

Because two is the new three.

Do not toss parachute up near trees or low overhangs.
Do not play in roads.
Play only in wide open areas.
Do not throw parachute at another person or animal.

She was not a wide open area.
She was a road.
I threw my parachute at her.
I threw my parachute at her animal.
She was a near tree.
A low overhang.

I tossed my parachute up.
I tossed my parachute near.
There was a brief falling, then

Ground.

SOLSTICE, WINTER

I am the one ending this year,
this dark. I am the one turning
the lights on again after having
turned them off, after having
left them on too long, all night long,
interrupting my sleep, then
stumbling in the false brightness.
After you pointed them out, I walked
across the room and turned them off.

Now the fire is bright against the house,
bright against the faces of women
throwing darkness into the fire,
sparking light.
Fire strewn.

I am the one strewning.
What was here to be done having finished.
I am the one.
Having finished.

We are silently in love with our children.

I type that into the computer and he watches me.

Mama, did I write that?

No but you inspired it.

When I kissed you and kissed you?

Yes, then.

I want to write a poem down about you, about the wisdom of you.

Did he really say that? Yes. I am writing it down.

Now I am reading it at 8:30 pm at the end of a day in which I do not feel very wise.

A dear friend said to me after Leo was born that we are lucky to be poets and mamas. Because if we're having a bad mama day, we could still have a good poet day. And if we're having a bad poet day, we could still have a good mama day.

I want the days I rock both.

Unlike today.

When nothing rocks. Even the unsinkable ship in the bathtub, does.

Mama, what if Gumby went down the drain?

Pokey would be so sad.

Mama look! Gumby went down the drain. Make Pokey cry.

I cry like I am an orange rubber pony whose best friend just went down the drain.

I am very convincing.

The way we fall says everything about our faith.
Leo falls like he's flying.
Our friend Micah throws him up in the air
and Leo leans into the air to make the fall even bigger.
Throws his arms back and his chest out and exhales.
He never short changes the fall worrying who will catch him.

Look out mama, there are 25 volcanoes interrupting!

I breathe and fall.

I cry and fall.

I sleep and fall.

I love and fall.

I fall and fall.

*Mama, the thing about me is that I can run through lava. It's easy.
I'll show you how I do it, watch me mama, watch me and then you
can do it too.*

The thing about me is that I follow directions well.

I run through the lava, laughing.

I don't even get burned at all.

Yellow. And you walking through the yellow.
This house. And you humming in this house.
Grey. And lights that shine through gray to guide me.

Ground, cold. And my feet on the cold ground, warm.
Now. The deep breath of now.
The urge to kiss what's coming.

May I create this space with abandon and acceptance.
Small and brief, if those are the materials available.
Fields and infinite, if those are the gifts arriving.

HUSH

The ocean has her head between my knees.
Along with every lover I've ever had.
Which isn't very many. So they almost all fit.

Here in the sun I am washing sadness down
with lemon and cayenne. I brewed it for my cold
but it seems to be taking care of everything.

I am puffy and salty and a little small.
A string of words falls from my fingers,
tickling up one arm then down the other.

When the snow comes to quiet me, I let it.
Everything is ok. Under a blanket of snow
everything can grow, still.

SOLSTICE, SUMMER

We have giant birds with red breasts in the blooming tree out front.
They land and the green bends. When you landed on my head my
heart my whole life bent and shimmered green and light to hold you
and I am permanently open now since you fell in and I fell in after
you and the world has woven itself into something like a net to
hammock us while we sleep and until we wake each morning we
wake each morning and say yes

Leo: Do you know Hannah Rand?

Me: I do. Is she in your band?

Leo: No. I'm in my band.

Me: Is there anyone else in your band?

Leo: A bunch of little Leo's.

Me: Is that the name of the band?

Leo: No. That's who's in the band.

Me: A bunch of little Leo's?

Leo: Yes.

Me: Do they all play the same instrument?

Leo: Yes.

Me: What instrument do they play?

Leo: Violin.

Me: So the whole band is little Leo's playing the violin?

Leo: Yes.

Turning and taking the blow, tires bent in, no paint chipped, no police, but a big tow truck, a gentle tow truck, a ride back and home, a lovely gesture, a body shop, a system, an insurance card, a number, another number, a tiny piece of paper with so many numbers, and a friend, an old friend, blocking the harsh wind.

I take the sugar hit for him, eating the sugar babies out of his birthday take-home gift bag, after he is in bed. I take as many hits as I can for him, his perfect 3-year old body hit-free.

I am not myself today. I am a parakeet. A Sea Otter. Little Ducky.
I am staring at salty waves, beyond
where private is safe, where public is open.
Because my son and my father.
My mother.
Because I don't have to know.

How can we feel strong?
Trusting something will not end, then
letting it end and trusting that.

BLACKBIRD

Blackbird, I followed you past five window screens
then watched you land and dive, and when

out of something to watch you through, I closed
my eyes to see you fly. We move in twos

and your lonely cry woke new the day, so it had
no choice but to break away and find another,

not merely an echo but a lover, hoping to go
where your wings know no other home.

Like you my road lies ceaselessly blue
and I question a sky unable to hide

the way we are born, this ache for more than
just ourselves to waken to. And someone

in our final hour who knows the total of
our lives, how high we flew and how we wept

when we met our other and we knew.

notes

APRIL
There are hundreds of ways to kneel and kiss the ground, Rumi

LANGUAGE ENTERS
Texts from "5" and "11" are from *Secrets of the Nest*, Joan Dunning

MY PLANS FOR TODAY
I a bell awakened, Denise Levertov

JULY
The directions for cutting glass were found in Henley's Twentieth Century
Book of Ten Thousand Formulas

APRIL, AGAIN
*I am the ant guy I am the guy who carries the rice I am the lemonade
drinking guy I'm the guy that pushes a ball with a stick I'm the guy who
takes care of these two things,* Leo Salach

*Eat the day. Eat the good day. Eat the really really really good day. Have a
good day,* Leo Salach

EMONKA (AN EMAIL SOMONKA)
1. emailed flower fact, *Mary Hawley*
2. emailed sunlight weight, *Mike Puican*
3. emailed crow quote, *Eileen Favorite*
4. Emailed roach fact, *Cecilia Pinto*
5. Emailed bat, dolphin, mosquito facts, *Chris Green*
6. Emailed mirror cells fact, *Alice George*

ALICE ASKS
All italicized questions, Alice George

SOLSTICE, WINTER
What was here to be done, having finished, Jane Hirshfield

cin salach has collaborated with a wide variety of artists for over twenty-five years and has performed in groups such as *The Loofah Method, Betty's Mouth* and *ten tongues.* Her first book, *Looking for a Soft Place to Land,* was published by Tia Chucha Press. She is honored that her second book makes her part of the Jackleg Press family. Her work has appeared on "This American Life" and "Oprah" and she has been widely published in journals and anthologies, including *Starting Today: 100 Poems for Obama's First 100 Days, Brute Neighbors: An Urban Nature Anthology,* and *Poetry Speaks: Spoken Word Revolution.*

Illinois Arts Council recipient, four-time Ragdale fellow and Emmy nominee for her voice-over and on-screen narration of the PBS documentary "From Schoolboy to Showgirl", cin lives in Andersonville with her young son, Leo, where her love of poetry, and her belief that it can change lives, has led her to launch **poemgrown**, helping people mark the most important occasions in their lives with poetry.

JackLeg Press
The Poetry Series

Hugh Behm-Steinberg
Barbara Cully
Neil de la Flor
D.C. Gonzalez-Prieto
Caroline Goodwin
Jennifer Harris
Meagan Lehr
Jenny Magnus
cin salach
Maureen Seaton
Kristine Snodgrass

jacklegpress.com

Made in the USA
Charleston, SC
04 May 2014